LEGO STAR WARS™

SECRETS
OF THE
DARK SIDE

Written by Matt Jones

Editor Matt Jones
Senior Designer Lauren Adams
Designers Sunita Gahir, Elena Jarmoskaite
Pre-production Producer Kavita Varma
Producer Louise Daly
Managing Editor Paula Regan
Design Manager Jo Connor
Publisher Julie Ferris
Art Director Lisa Lanzarini
Publishing Director Simon Beecroft

First American Edition, 2017
Published in the United States by DK Publishing
345 Hudson Street, New York, New York 10014
DK, a Division of Penguin Random House LLC

Page design copyright © 2018 Dorling Kindersley Limited

17 18 19 20 10 9 8 7 6 5 4 3 2 1
007–299071–March/17

A catalog record for this book is available from the Library of Congress.

ISBN: 978-1-4654-6336-4 (Paperback)
ISBN: 978-1-4654-6337-1 (Hardback)

DK books are available at special discounts when purchased in bulk for sales promotions,
premiums, fund-raising, or educational use. For details, contact: DK Publishing Special
Markets, 345 Hudson Street, New York, New York 10014
SpecialSales@dk.com

Printed and bound in China

A WORLD OF IDEAS:
SEE ALL THERE IS TO KNOW

www.LEGO.com/starwars
www.starwars.com
www.dk.com

Contents

The Force

The Force is a great power.
It has a light side and a
dark side.
The light side is used for good.

Darth Vader

The dark side is used for evil.
Luke Skywalker is a Jedi.
He uses the light side.
Darth Vader is a Sith.
He uses the dark side.

Luke Skywalker

Darth Sidious

Darth Sidious leads the Sith.
He does not like the Jedi.
He wants to control the galaxy!

Stormtrooper

Stormtrooper Sergeant

Snowtrooper

Sandtrooper

Armored troops

The Sith have many troops.
They wear different armor.
They can fight in the snow,
sand, and water.

Shoretrooper   Scout Trooper

Darth Maul

Darth Maul is a scary Sith!
He is from the planet Dathomir.

Maul has horns on his head.
He has a special lightsaber
with two red blades.

Count Dooku

Count Dooku was once a Jedi.
Now he has joined the Sith.

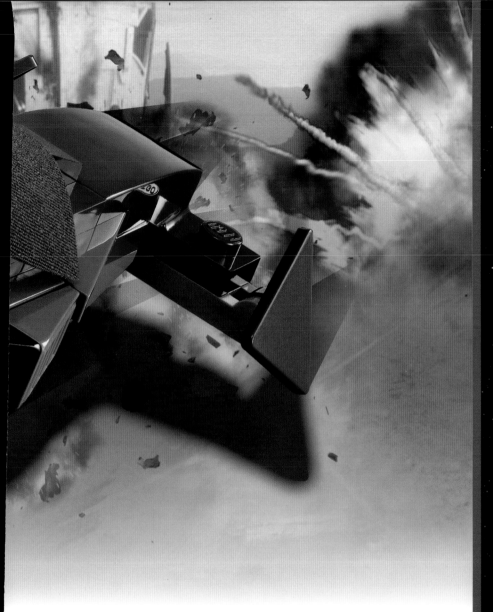

The Jedi want to find him.
He escapes from the Jedi
on his speeder bike.

14 Anakin Skywalker

Asajj Ventress

Asajj Ventress is a strong Sith.
She uses two red lightsabers.
She tries to defeat Anakin
Skywalker in battle.

TIE Interceptor

Speedy vehicles

The Sith and their troops
have lots of vehicles.
They can battle in space,
the air, or on the ground.

Star Destroyer

AT-AT

Darth Vader

The powerful Darth Vader
was once hurt in battle.
Now he has to wear a suit
of armor to protect his body.

Kylo Ren

Kylo Ren uses the dark side
of the Force.
Kylo wants to rule the galaxy.

Kylo Ren

Rey uses the light side
of the Force.
Can Rey stop Kylo Ren?

Rey

Quiz

1. Who leads the Sith?

2. Why does Darth Vader wear a suit of armor?

3. Which Sith uses two lightsabers?

4. Who has horns on his head?

5. Who escapes from the Jedi on a speeder bike?

Answers on page 23

Index

Answers to the quiz on page 22

1. Darth Sidious
2. To protect his body
3. Asajj Ventress
4. Darth Maul
5. Count Dooku

23

A Note to Parents

THIS BOOK is part of an exciting four-level reading series for children, developing the habit of reading widely for both pleasure and information. The series is designed in conjunction with leading literacy experts, including Dr. Linda Gambrell, Distinguished Professor of Education at Clemson University. Dr. Gambrell has served as President of the National Reading Conference, the College Reading Association, and the International Reading Association.

Beautiful illustrations and superb full-color photographs combine with engaging, easy-to-read stories to offer a fresh approach to each subject in the series. Each book is guaranteed to capture a child's interest while developing his or her reading skills, general knowledge, and love of reading.

The four levels of reading books are aimed at different reading abilities, enabling you to choose the books that are exactly right for your child:

Level 1: Learning to read
Level 2: Beginning to read
Level 3: Beginning to read alone
Level 4: Reading alone

The "normal" age at which a child begins to read can be anywhere from three to eight years old. Adult participation through the lower levels is very helpful for providing encouragement, discussing storylines, and sounding out unfamiliar words.

No matter which level you select, you can be sure that you are helping your child learn to read, then read to learn!

Discover the dark side of the Force!

Meet the villains of the LEGO® *Star Wars*™ galaxy. Can they be stopped?

LEARN TO READ, THEN READ TO LEARN!

Engaging topics and fun, interactive pages build reading skills • Developed in consultation with leading literacy experts • Helps build a lifelong love of reading

A level for every reader

LEVEL 1 LEARNING TO READ

LEVEL 2 BEGINNING TO READ

LEVEL 3 BEGINNING TO READ ALONE

LEVEL 4 READING ALONE

Look out for other great titles!

$3.99 USA
$4.99 Canada

www.dk.com

© & TM 2018 LUCASFILM LTD.
starwars.com

I S B N 978-1-4654-6336-4   Printed in China

5 0 3 9 9

9 781465 463364

I PLEDGE ALLEGIANCE

REVISED 2ND EDITION

BY JUNE SWANSON
PICTURES BY RICK HANSON

SCHOLASTIC